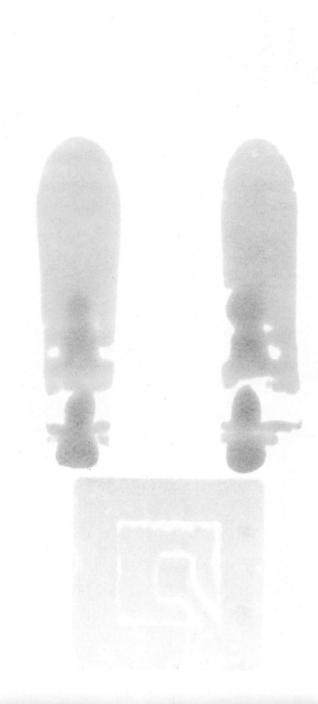

GO OUTSIDE

AND COME BACK BETTER

GO OUTSIDE
AND COME BACK BETTER

Benefits from Nature That Everyone Should Know

Ron Lizzi

River Stream Media
Bethany, Connecticut

GO OUTSIDE AND COME BACK BETTER
Benefits from Nature That Everyone Should Know

Published by River Stream Media
RiverStreamMedia.com

Cover photo: Hiker views Corona Arch, Utah

Publisher's Cataloging-in-Publication Data

Lizzi, Ronald.
   Go outside and come back better : benefits from nature that everyone should know / Ron Lizzi.
      p. cm.
   Includes index.
   ISBN 978-1-939435-78-1
   1. Outdoor recreation. 2. Travel—Psychological aspects. 3. Nature—Psychological aspects. 4. Parks—United States—Pictorial works.   I. Title.
   BF353.5.N37 L59 2013
   155.9—dc23

                                                                                    2012922078

Printed in China by Everbest through Four Colour Print Group, Louisville, Kentucky

10 9 8 7 6 5 4 3 2 1

This book is dedicated to you, the reader.
I hope this will become clear.

Acknowledgments

Beyond the people who aided in the writing of this book, I must thank those who contributed to the experiences discussed herein.

First, I want to acknowledge all the women and men who have ever worked on America's public lands. This includes the five agencies that administer federal lands: the National Park Service, the U.S. Forest Service, the U.S. Fish and Wildlife Service, the Bureau of Land Management, and the Bureau of Reclamation, plus the U.S. Army Corps of Engineers, which also makes some of its properties available for recreation. Of course I also include state, county, and municipal parks, and Native American tribal parks. And finally there are many private organizations like The Nature Conservancy and the National Audubon Society that conserve lands and open them to the public.

Yes, some of the employees of these organizations get paid to do their jobs, but let's face it, nobody gets rich being a park ranger, so the element of public service shouldn't be overlooked.

Before we had parks, there were explorers like John Muir, who possessed the curiosity to discover nature's treasures and the wisdom to advocate their preservation. We are all indebted to them.

Recognition also goes to the citizens of the Internet—all the shutterbugs, birders, waterfall nuts, outdoors lovers—who share their photos, reviews, and tips. They have helped me make the most of my trips, and I hope to do the same for others with this book and its companion website: GoOutsideBook.com.

My gratitude extends to the emergency and medical personnel of Columbia County, Pennsylvania, and Geisinger Medical Center, who rescued and fixed me. The most perilous part of my trips is . . . highway travel.

I also wish to recognize Georgia Tech and the West Hartford Public Schools, where I learned to learn, and my former employer, Timex Corporation, which unwittingly encouraged me to go outside.

Lastly, I give heartfelt thanks to my friends and family for their support and encouragement (or tolerance) in all my endeavors.

Contents

1

Matterdays and the Day Stone Balance

What makes a good life? If I had a bunch of letters after my name (PhD/MD/PsyD), I might give a complicated answer, making you regret considering the question. Having no letters after my name, I offer a simple answer: a good life consists of a lot of good days.

We all know when we've had a good or a bad day. Suppose you kept track. But not like a CPA would—no letters, remember?

Suppose you had a balance. Picture a seesaw (*teeter-totter* in some places). This balance represents your life.

Now imagine that at the end of every day, you placed a stone on the balance. For a good day, you would put the stone on the right side. So, a day you received praise at work might look like this:

The better the day, the farther to the right the stone would go. The day of your child's birth, a day of great excitement and joy, might yield this:

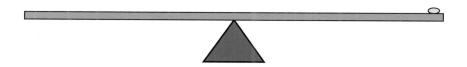

A bad day—say, a day on which you lost your job—would result in a stone on the left side.

Of course the majority of days are so-so, and on those days the stones go near the middle, where they have little effect on the balance.

After a while, your day stone balance takes shape, ending up looking like this:

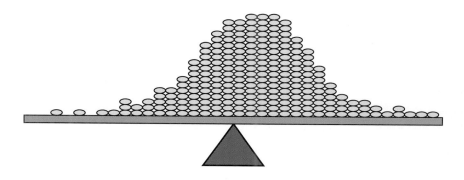

The quality of your life would be determined by how strongly the balance would tip to one side or the other. If the stones tip it slightly downward on the right, you have a good life; strongly on the right indicates a better life; on the left, not so good.

But wait, a lifetime has thousands of days, most of which are quickly forgotten or lose any relevance to your present-day life. For example, when you were two years old (or thereabouts), you had a triumphant day, pooping in that odd porcelain contraption instead of your diaper. But that doesn't count. Sure, it was certainly a critical step in your development—consider where you'd be without that skill—but you get no stone for that day. Or that time you spent twenty minutes on hold for customer service, having punched your way through countless menus and listened to an incessant loop of irritating music, only to be disconnected? Well, maybe that day's stone didn't disappear but rather just shifted a bit toward the center, becoming less bad over time as it faded from memory.

Conversely, days that seemed completely insignificant at the time could prove important. Maybe nothing remarkable happened, but simply waking up next to your life partner or going to a job you love was enough to put that day and many others like it on the "good" side.

In short, some days matter and some don't. The day stone balance only holds stones for what I call *matterdays*.

So, your life has now been reduced to a balance and a pile of stones. You're excited, no doubt.

Myriad books by people with letters after their names tell you how to improve your family life/working life/financial life/spiritual life/love life. Such improvements would certainly yield more stones on the right side of the day stone balance. That's wonderful. But that's not what this book is about.

Now, anyone with advanced seesaw knowledge understands that the farther you are from the middle of the seesaw, the greater your impact on the balance. A kid sitting on one end can balance out two kids seated on the opposite side but closer to the middle. So, applying that principle to the day stone balance, a great matterday or an awful matterday will have a larger impact than a bunch of marginally good or bad matterdays.

Instead of aiming to improve your life by making all of your future days slightly better, you ought to be able to do the trick with some number of great matterdays, especially if those days were so positive, they diminished your negative perception of other days. *That's* what this book is about.

OK, fine, you may be thinking. But exactly how do you go about *having* those great matterdays, days that substantially improve your life? You can only have so many weddings, births, graduations, house closings, and promotions. For those fortunate enough to have them—and many people are not so fortunate—such days may be once-in-a-lifetime events, the culmination of months or years of effort, and their rarity is what helps to make them special. Other great matterdays are tied to luck or events beyond your control, like a chance meeting or a championship for your team. It seems that you're destined to have a limited number of great matterdays. You dream of those days and wait patiently . . . or impatiently.

But what if you could create great matterdays at will, without courtship, morning sickness, studying, or overtime? What if you could produce them by yourself, without depending on a boss, a loved one, or a group of sweaty people in uniforms? What if you didn't need luck?

You can certainly create good days by doing things you enjoy, but to create a great matterday—something significant—seems difficult if not impossible.

What makes a day a great matterday is its positive impact on your life. You can have a good day spending time with friends or enjoying a hobby, but will it really have much impact on you? Will you be different afterward? If not, it's simply another good day, matterday or not.

A great matterday is one you'll remember for its effect on you. Whether the day's details—the date or the exact location—stick in your mind is unimportant. What matters is that you remember what you experienced, how you felt, and what you thought. A great matterday is one of discovery, one from which you found a new feeling, a new understanding, or a new outlook—a day you were moved, changed.

Suppose I told you that there are places where great matterdays happen, and you have only to go there and experience them. That if you spent enough time at these places, you could actually shift the balance of your life. You'd be skeptical, right? I would have been too, before it unexpectedly happened to me.

Such days are available from nature. Let me show you.

2

Nature's Offerings

To see how nature can impact your life, you must first have a sense of what nature offers. Unfortunately, many of us *don't* have that, and often we don't even realize it.

Even if you have never visited any national parks that showcase nature, you would probably consider yourself aware of them. You've undoubtedly seen pictures of them, whether on a calendar, a travel guide, or postcards from Aunt Millie. You think they're nice. You'd like to go sometime. Maybe next year. Maybe when you retire.

But do you really know what's out there, how striking and amazingly diverse the scenery is? Do you believe that just being out in nature could profoundly impact your life? Probably not.

In spite of our ever-increasing population, U.S. national park visitation has actually declined in recent years. Furthermore, Americans are taking fewer vacations longer than one week, opting instead for short ones or occasional days off. If you're contributing to these trends (either by choice or by necessity), you really should know what you're missing.

Words and pictures can hardly do the parks justice, but allow me to give you a sampling of the wonderful places available to you. You may discover that you don't know America as well as you thought you did.

For example, you might recognize Arizona.

Cathedral Rock and Oak Creek viewed from the Crescent Moon Picnic Area—
Coconino National Forest, Arizona

This and other stunning rock formations help bring millions of tourists annually to the
nearby city of Sedona, Arizona.

But what about Michigan?

Grand Portal and Lake Superior—Pictured Rocks National Lakeshore, Michigan

This park features 12 miles (19 kilometers) of colorful sandstone cliffs, up to 200 feet (60 meters) high, along the southern shore of Lake Superior, largest of the Great Lakes.

How well do you know Texas?

Bald cypresses with Spanish moss in Saw Mill Pond—Caddo Lake State Park, Texas

Surprises abound across the country. Vast sand dunes, the tallest in North America, reside in Colorado.

Dune field and Cleveland Peak—Great Sand Dunes National Park & Preserve, Colorado

Geologists believe these dunes, as tall as 750 feet (228 meters), formed from opposing winds that carried sand left over from a huge lakebed that once covered the area. The dunes, which geologists believe started forming around 440,000 years ago, are still slowly growing.

Sandstone arches grace Tennessee and Kentucky.

Hike beneath South Arch—Big South Fork National River & Recreation Area, Tennessee.

South Arch spans 135 feet (41 meters) and rises 103 feet (31 meters). Combining South Arch with its smaller companion, North Arch, the Twin Arches are among the largest natural bridges in the world.

Huge boulders, delivered by an ancient glacier, rest—in this case seemingly rather precariously—in New Jersey.

Tripod Rock—Pyramid Mountain Natural Historic Area, Morris County, New Jersey

This 160-ton (145-tonne) boulder is what's called a *glacial erratic*—a rock that was transported from elsewhere by a glacier and deposited in the landscape. Over 18,000 years ago the Wisconsin Glacier carried this rock to its resting place atop three smaller boulders.

A lush canyon, the deepest one east of the Mississippi River, cuts across Alabama.

Little River Canyon viewed from the Wolf Creek Overlook (400 feet / 122 meters above Little River)—Little River Canyon National Preserve, Alabama

And a variety of stone creatures populate Utah.

Red Canyon hoodoos (rock columns)—Dixie National Forest, Utah

In school, you may have learned to locate West Virginia on a map and identify Charleston as its capital. But you probably weren't taught about the natural beauty of this state or shown the great rocks that once formed part of a shoal on the edge of an ancient ocean.

Seneca Rocks with flowering eastern redbud and black mustard wildflowers—Spruce Knob–Seneca Rocks National Recreation Area, Monongahela National Forest, West Virginia

Perhaps you've sung of America's "purple mountain majesties." But have you actually *seen* any?

Harvest moon rises over Vermilion Peak (elevation 13,894 feet / 4,235 meters) with alpenglow—San Juan National Forest, Colorado

As for America's parks, you've probably heard of Yosemite National Park.

El Capitan (left) and Half Dome (right) at sunrise—Yosemite National Park, California

But do you know Lassen Volcanic National Park?

Cinder Cone—Lassen Volcanic National Park, California

A few centuries ago a volcanic eruption created the cone, which is 700 feet (213 meters) high.

And what about Delaware Water Gap National Recreation Area?

Silver Thread Falls (80 feet / 24 meters high)—Delaware Water Gap National Recreation Area, Pennsylvania

Some of the most beautiful places in the country aren't national parks but other federal lands.

Mount Hood (elevation 11,239 feet / 3,426) and Lost Lake—Mount Hood National Forest, Oregon

Mount Hood is a volcanic member of the Cascade Range, which stretches from Northern California to British Columbia, Canada.

Or state parks.

Gnarled live oak on Driftwood Beach at sunrise—Jekyll Island State Park, Georgia

Most oaks are deciduous, but this evergreen species is called a live oak because it retains at least some foliage and looks alive in winter.

Or even county or municipal parks.

Rock cliff by the Eau Claire River surrounded by fall foliage—Dells of the Eau Claire Park, Marathon County, Wisconsin

Many natural treasures are found in Native American tribal parks.

Passage in Lower Antelope Canyon ("Hasdestwazi" in the Navajo language)—Lake Powell Navajo Tribal Park, Arizona

The Navajo Nation, which covers an area larger than the state of West Virginia, is home to a wealth of spectacular and unspoiled scenery.

Despite the dizzying array of parks available, some people have yet to develop much interest in nature or act on what interest they *do* have. Some even say, "I don't really like the outdoors."

Think about that statement. Taken literally, it's unfathomable, as if the outdoors is merely that unavoidable space between buildings. Life without the outdoors—not even a view through a window—is often called *prison.*

At the other end of the spectrum, think about paradise. You don't envision a windowless room, do you?

Coconut palms along a rocky shore and black-sand beach—Wai'anapanapa State Park, Hawaii

If you had the chance to visit paradise or heaven, would you? Are you thinking you'll get another chance later? What if you reach the Pearly Gates, and Saint Peter says, "Hey, you had plenty of opportunities to spend time in heavenly places down there. Sorry."

Upper (1,430 feet / 436 meters high) and Lower (320 feet / 98 meters high) Yosemite Falls—Yosemite National Park, California

Maybe you thought such magnificent places were limited to exclusive resorts that require wealth to access, when they are in fact available to everyone. Taxpayers often wonder where their money goes, never considering that they actually own a share of some prime vacation property.

McWay Falls (80 feet / 24 meters high)—Julia Pfeiffer Burns State Park, California

McWay Falls is the only coastal waterfall in California. At high tide it spills directly into the Pacific Ocean.

Paradise would be enough for some, but your opportunities don't end there. If you could spend a day on another planet, would you go?

Badlands—Toadstool Geologic Park, Nebraska

The badlands, which include rock formations that resemble toadstools, were formed from millions of years' worth of river sediment deposits combined with ash from volcanic eruptions, followed by erosion that continues to this day.

If that planet doesn't suit you, perhaps this one would.

Cliffs and spires of Cathedral Gorge—Cathedral Gorge State Park, Nevada

From mountains to badlands to rocky coastline, many of nature's most striking features have connections to volcanoes. That includes Cathedral Gorge's formations, which are made of volcanic ash sediments from an ancient lake. After the lake drained, the exposed landscape was carved by rain and wind.

If you could explore the earth's hidden underground chambers, would you?

Twin Domes (42 feet / 13 meters high) and Giant Dome (62 feet / 19 meters high)—Carlsbad Caverns National Park, New Mexico

These huge stalagmites are among the highlights of the Big Room, a 14-acre (5.7-hectare) cave that lies 750 feet (229 meters) underground. Visitors may tour this wonder on their own, a rarity for caves.

What nature offers you is in part determined by how you view it. Perhaps you've admired works of art in museums. Suppose you considered the parks to be museums, with both permanent exhibits . . .

Full moon setting over Chimney Rock (325 feet / 99 meters high) at sunrise—Chimney Rock National Historic Site, Nebraska

Chimney Rock served as a landmark for nineteenth-century pioneers bound for the West.

. . . and ones that change daily.

Rippled dune—Bruneau Dunes State Park, Idaho

Do you see art in nature, paintings on an infinite canvas?

Pond reflection—Weir Farm National Historic Site, Connecticut

Painter J. Alden Weir acquired this farm in 1882 and created a place of inspiration for generations of artists.

Or sculptures in a vast garden?

Cap rock formations (about 9 feet / 3 meters tall)—Theodore Roosevelt National Park, North Dakota

These mushroomlike pillars are formed when the relatively hard sandstone atop the formations shields the underlying clay from rain erosion.

Maybe your interests lie with museums that showcase relics of bygone eras.

Petrified logs of the Crystal Forest—Petrified Forest National Park, Arizona

Approximately 225 million years ago, floods buried whole logs in river sediment that cut off the oxygen that would have allowed them to decay normally. Instead, over hundreds or thousands of years, the organic material was replaced by minerals like silica from volcanic ash, yielding colorful quartz logs. Over time the brittle crystal fractured easily and cleanly into chunks that appear sawed off.

Or is it architecture that appeals to you? Do you enjoy marveling at skyscrapers?

The Titan (900 feet / 274 meters high) at sunset—Fisher Towers Recreation Site, Utah

Perhaps you love animals.

Desert bighorn sheep—Anza–Borrego Desert State Park, California

Or flowers.

Great egret and bur marigolds—Cypress Island Preserve, Louisiana

This preserve, which is open to the public, is owned and maintained by The Nature Conservancy, a nonprofit conservation organization.

Sometimes the attraction isn't only what you can see *in* a park but what you can see *from* it. The remoteness of some parks offers something hidden from most of the population: a brilliant night sky, particularly around a new moon, when the Milky Way appears.

It's ten o'clock; do you know where your galaxy is?

Jumbo Rocks beneath a starry sky—Joshua Tree National Park, California

These places may be as unfamiliar to you as they were to me not so long ago. After years as a homebody, I finally discovered nature's offerings when I parlayed a business trip to Northern California into a cheap and convenient opportunity to hike in some national parks for the first time.

My excursion to Yosemite, Sequoia, and Kings Canyon National Parks left me stunned; I had never seen such gorgeous and amazing places. But beyond my astonishment, I was frankly somewhat embarrassed. I thought: "How did I not know about these places, how incredible they are? Did I miss that day in school when the topic was covered? Where have I been? Spending precious vacation days spreading broadleaf weed killer on the lawn? Am I nuts? What if I hadn't needed to go to California on business?"

Liberty Cap and Nevada Fall (594 feet / 181 meters high) viewed from the John Muir Trail—Yosemite National Park, California

Unfamiliarity with these natural places is quite common and understandable, though. Parks have no publicists or marketing machines behind them; no big corporations profit from your visits to public parks. You won't see any TV commercials featuring a sexy model in front of Yosemite Falls. Yellowstone has no catchy slogan, no jingle. No Super Bowl victor has ever shouted, "I'm going to the Everglades!"

As a result, if you happen to be in Vegas, you will likely stay in Vegas, unaware of the fantastic national and state parks within a few hours' drive.

Early morning at Elephant Rock—Valley of Fire State Park, Nevada

This park, an easy one-hour drive northeast of Las Vegas, provides a wonderland of colorful sandstone formations.

We have become such consumers of advertising that we frequently know little about things that are not pitched to us, no matter how incredible or beneficial they are. We are thus conditioned to disregard anything unaccompanied by promotion.

So you may recognize plenty of stars of the entertainment world but not many stars of the natural world.

Morning Glory Pool—Yellowstone National Park, Wyoming

The pool is a hot spring inhabited by bacteria that give the water its color.

No doubt you're familiar with many top performers in the music business, but do you know *this* enduring rock star?

Delicate Arch (opening 45 feet / 14 meters high) at sunset—Arches National Park, Utah

This park contains over two thousand sandstone arches, although only a small fraction are accessible to visitors.

Perhaps you follow the Cardinals, Falcons, or Penguins, but can you spot a cormorant?

Double-crested cormorant—Everglades National Park, Florida

The park's Anhinga Trail provides remarkably close views of many birds—including egrets, herons, ibises, wood storks, anhingas, and cormorants—as well as alligators.

Maybe you've been captivated by the exotic lands in movies or video games, but have you explored *real* dramatic scenery?

Cross Fissures View—Black Canyon of the Gunnison National Park, Colorado

While Arizona's Grand Canyon garners attention for its size, Black Canyon displays its own grandeur, with sheer walls that plunge up to 2,722 feet (829 meters) down to the roaring Gunnison River.

How many ads have you seen for theme parks while seeing none for public parks, where the theme is "nature, beauty, and history"?

Yahoo Falls (113 feet / 34 meters high)—Big South Fork National River & Recreation Area, Kentucky

With so many options competing for your leisure time, it's easy to overlook nature. And a hectic lifestyle makes it tempting to catch up on chores or simply relax. But great matterdays rarely result from sleeping late or just doing nothing. Nor do they come from such necessities as running errands or caring for the house—as if confusing *house* with *spouse*.

Window Arch at sunrise—City of Rocks National Reserve, Idaho

3

Emotional Inspiration

"OK," you say, "there are lots of interesting and scenic places to see—many more than I knew—but how do these places make a difference in my life?" Well, the impact comes in two forms, both inspirational, though one is purely emotional while the other more thoughtful. Leaving the thoughtful form for the next chapter, let's explore the emotional side by continuing our tour of American parks.

I'd like to have a virtual friend join us for the remainder of this virtual trip. His name is John Muir. If you've been to certain national parks, you may have bumped into him, so to speak. John possessed keen insight and a way with words, and his thoughts have graced many park plaques. Having visited the parks, I've encountered his quotations so many times in different places that I've felt like saying, "Get a job!"

Actually, John—who lived from 1838 to 1914—had a number of jobs (sheepherder, rancher, writer) and hobbies (inventor, geologist, botanist). But he had one overriding mission: to protect wilderness. His passion for nature, expressed through his influential writings, made him a leader in conservation, and he successfully advocated for the establishment of several of America's first national parks. Although never part of the U.S. government, John Muir is often called the father of the national park system.

Unfortunately, living in the twenty-first century, I couldn't get away with saying the things he did without having people look at me funny. So I'll occasionally call on him to work his poetic magic. In fact, he's going to kick off this next leg of our journey.

Climb the mountains and get their good tidings.

Mount Rainier (elevation 14,410 feet / 4,392 meters), with Indian paintbrush and Sitka valerian wildflowers, viewed from Pinnacle Peak Saddle—Mount Rainier National Park, Washington

On a clear day Mount Rainier, a huge volcano and the highest peak in the Cascade Range, can be seen from Portland, Oregon, 100 miles (161 kilometers) away.

Nature's peace will flow into you as sunshine flows into trees.

Redwoods of the Boy Scout Tree Trail—Jedediah Smith Redwoods State Park, California, and part of Redwood National and State Parks

The redwoods of the California coast, the world's tallest trees, can reach 367 feet (112 meters) and routinely live for centuries.

The winds will blow their own freshness into you, and the storms their energy, . . .

Winds whip Lake Michigan in front of Fisherman's Island as a storm clears—Fisherman's Island State Park, Michigan

. . . while cares will drop off like autumn leaves.

—John Muir

Fallen leaves carpet the rocky banks of Dry Creek—Fillmore Glen State Park, New York

John recognized the profound emotional impact of nature on the human psyche.

In everyday life we bounce between familiar places: home to work to shopping. So it is with our emotions. We go from stress to satisfaction to annoyance to contentment to worry to relaxation. Occasional events add spice to our emotional stew, but with a largely unchanging collection of ingredients, it's hard to cook up a great matterday.

But when we go outside those familiar sets of places and emotions, enduring memories are made. Some parks evoke an emotion unknown to those stuck in the daily grind, one I call *awezure,* a combination of awe and pleasure (the *Z* clarifies pronunciation and makes the word reminiscent of *azure,* the color of a clear sky).

Colorado River (1,100 feet / 335 meters below) at Horseshoe Bend—Glen Canyon National Recreation Area, Arizona

While Grand Canyon National Park caters to its millions of visitors, upstream from there, near Page, Arizona, Horseshoe Bend is heralded by only a simple road sign on Highway 89. There are no facilities here, just a small parking area, which is the trailhead for a short hike to this mesmerizing view.

But awezure really includes more than feelings of awe and pleasure; it also encompasses feelings of harmony and peace.

> *Every day opens and closes like a flower, noiseless, effortless. Divine peace glows on all the majestic landscape, like the silent enthusiastic joy that sometimes transfigures a noble human face.*
>
> —John Muir

Bullhead Pond at sunrise—DeSoto National Wildlife Refuge, Iowa

Such feelings are derived from nature's projection of strength and reliability.

So often we suffer disappointment. Relationships fail. Plans go awry. Misfortune befalls. We need things we can depend on, and nature delivers, proving itself worthy of the honorific *mother*. The sun rises and sets, the rivers flow, the flowers bloom, and the rocks stand tall.

> *There is a love of wild nature in everybody, an ancient mother love ever showing itself whether recognized or no, and however covered by cares and duties.*
>
> —John Muir

Nez Perce Spire—Bitterroot National Forest, Montana

Yet with awezure's peace, there is never a sense of idleness. Nature's energy and dynamism impart the promise that we are witness to a grand show.

Harding Icefield (300 square miles / 777 square kilometers) flows into Exit Glacier— Kenai Fjords National Park, Alaska

The Harding Icefield receives, on average, 60 feet (18 meters) of snow per year. Over the course of years, the snow, which is 80 percent air, compacts to become glacial ice, which is less than 20 percent air.

The mountain peaks and ridges that poke through the ice are called *nunataks*.

Nature is ever at work building and pulling down, creating and destroying, keeping everything whirling and flowing, allowing no rest but in rhythmical motion, chasing everything in endless song out of one beautiful form into another.

—John Muir

Holei Sea Arch (about 90 feet / 27 meters tall), lava rock carved by the surf—Hawaii Volcanoes National Park, Hawaii

Mystery often colors the feeling. Nature fosters curiosity and invites study, denying understanding to the casual observer.

Stone Mountain—Stone Mountain State Park, North Carolina

Awezure stems from a combination of senses, not just sight. The scent of wildflowers, the sound of the pounding surf, and the feel of a cool breeze on the skin can all contribute to this unique emotion.

Sunset over Massachusetts Bay—Cape Cod National Seashore, Massachusetts

To feel awezure is to see the world as a vast wellspring of life, not only for its plants and animals but also for its rocks and rivers, its storms and seas—features not alive but surely lively.

Here is a cascade two hundred feet wide, half a mile long, glancing this way and that, filled with bounce and dance and joyous hurrah, yet earnest as a tempest, and singing like angels loose on a frolic from heaven.

—John Muir

Step Falls—Step Falls Preserve, Maine

This preserve, which is open to the public, is owned and maintained by The Nature Conservancy, a nonprofit conservation organization.

When you were little, you used to get so excited. When you went someplace special like the beach, the zoo, or an amusement park, what did you do when you got there? You *ran*. It wasn't that the object of your desire was going to escape; you just couldn't get to it fast enough. The excitement flowed right through your little legs. When you had to wait for *impossibly* slow adults and couldn't run ahead, you expended the energy by hopping in place. And if a fence or railing separated you from the prime attraction, you pressed up against it to be as close as possible, eyes wide and unblinking.

You're older now, more controlled, but that little kid is still in you. When you feel impending awezure, you might not run or hop, but you may find yourself walking a little faster, propelled by your quickening heartbeat.

Bryce Amphitheater viewed from Bryce Point—Bryce Canyon National Park, Utah

Despite its name, the park is actually not a canyon, which is defined as a narrow valley between two cliffs, cut by flowing water. Erosion from water and ice sculpted the hoodoos, which are up to 150 feet (45 meters) tall.

And when you reach that special place, like a thirsty soul who has just received a glass of water, you feel your excitement turn into refreshment as you drink in the sights and sounds and scents.

Big Sur coast at sunset—Garrapata State Park, California

These feelings appear so rarely—if ever—in everyday life that many of us have unconsciously altered our emotional scales to accommodate a smaller range. Have you ever tossed around the word "breathtaking" without actually *having* your breath taken?

Crater Lake, Wizard Island (a volcanic cinder cone), and Llao Rock—Crater Lake National Park, Oregon

Crater Lake, the deepest lake in the United States, fills a caldera (volcanic basin) that formed after an eruption caused the collapse of Mount Mazama 7,700 years ago.

Some park visits yield an emotional impact so powerful that "sight-seeing" fails to adequately describe the experience. "Placefeeling" fits better.

Maroon Bells (elevation 14,156 feet / 4,315 meters) and Maroon Creek with golden aspens—Maroon Bells Scenic Area, White River National Forest, Colorado

Everybody needs beauty as well as bread, places . . . where Nature may heal and cheer and give strength to body and soul alike.

—John Muir

We all know the importance of a balanced diet for a healthy body, but the mind needs a balanced diet too. Has your soul received the recommended daily allowance of beauty, of inspiration, of awezure?

Mount Moran (elevation 12,605 feet / 3,842 meters) and aspens reflected in the Snake River at Oxbow Bend—Grand Teton National Park, Wyoming

No healthy man who delivers himself into the hands of Nature can possibly doubt the doubleness of his life. Soul and body receive separate nourishment and separate exercise, and speedily reach a stage of development wherein each is easily known apart from the other.

—John Muir

Bald cypress in Trap Pond with fall color—Trap Pond State Park, Delaware

This park includes the northernmost stand of this wetland tree.

Of course some of these places may not seem so beautiful to you. Beauty is, after all, in the eye of the beholder. But isn't your enjoyment of life at least somewhat determined by how broad your definition of beauty is? You see beauty here.

Silver Cascade (640 feet / 195 meters high) in early autumn—Crawford Notch State Park, New Hampshire

But do you see it here?

Flowstone wall (32 feet / 10 meters high) in Cathedral Caverns—Cathedral Caverns State Park, Alabama

Flowstones are sheetlike deposits of calcite formed by water flowing down the walls or along the floors of a cave.

Or here?

Joshua trees at sunset—Joshua Tree National Park, California

Not truly a tree but a type of yucca, Joshua trees in the park reach up to 40 feet (12 meters) tall and may be hundreds of years old.

Beauty is not always obvious; sometimes it must be sought out.

Trio of colorful sea stars revealed by low tide at Ruby Beach—Olympic National Park, Washington

Commonly known as starfish, these creatures, which are not fish at all, have been renamed by marine scientists. Approximately two thousand sea star species inhabit the world's oceans.

Often beauty is in plain view, awaiting your notice.

Immature spruce cones (0.8 inches / 2.0 centimeters long) at Schoodic Point—
Acadia National Park, Maine

And finding beauty is not simply a matter of knowing *where* to look but also *when*.

Cedar Falls (50 feet / 15 meters high) after heavy springtime rains—Hocking Hills State Park, Ohio

This waterfall is dry or a trickle much of the year. In spring, rain and snowmelt bring the park to life.

Is it time for you to consider a different definition of *happy hour*?

View through Mesa Arch at sunrise—Canyonlands National Park, Utah

Those who have witnessed horrific scenes lament that they will always carry the images with them. Sublime scenery can similarly leave a lasting impression. Certainly no single positive image imparts the impact of one from a tragedy, but when you've beheld magnificent scenery repeatedly and accumulated enough images to cause you to see the world as an exquisite place, the effect can be every bit as powerful and permanent.

Mount Shuksan (elevation 9,131 feet / 2,783 meters) and Picture Lake—Mount Baker Wilderness, Mount Baker–Snoqualmie National Forest, Washington

These beautiful days must enrich all my life. They do not exist as mere pictures—maps hung upon the walls of memory to brighten at times when touched by association or will, only to sink again like a landscape in the dark; but they saturate themselves into every part of the body and live always.

—John Muir

Bash Bish Falls (50 feet / 15 meters high) after a snowstorm—Bash Bish Falls State Park, Massachusetts

If the parks can enhance or expand your appreciation of the world, your day stone balance has been tipped.

Storm clouds approach Tent Rocks—Kasha–Katuwe Tent Rocks National Monument, New Mexico

4
Thoughtful Inspiration

Fantastic scenery alone would be enough to make outstanding parks worth visiting, but there is more.

When we are with Nature, we are awake, and we discover many interesting things and reach many a mark we are not aiming at.

—John Muir

The idea that America hosts myriad parks of surpassing beauty that evoke pleasant emotions should not surprise you, but what might be unexpected is the many life lessons these places provide. Their inspirational messages may be ones you've heard or read before, or perhaps they seem obvious, but they are delivered *differently* in the parks. When these messages are embodied in nature as opposed to mere words, they resonate and remain with you. You remember that tree, that animal, that scene.

Remember, matterdays have a lasting impact on your life. Since by definition learning is change, when you learn nature's lessons, you are changed.

Washington's Mount St. Helens stood as a scenic gem. Like its sister peaks in the Cascade Range, it owed its conical grace to a volcanic heritage.

On May 18, 1980, Mount St. Helens transformed itself from majestic mountain to violent volcano, erupting with a force greater than 500 Hiroshima bombs. The north face of the mountain collapsed, and debris blasted across the land at over 600 miles (960 kilometers) per hour. The eruption left the mountain 1,300 feet (400 meters) lower, destroyed nearly 150 square miles (400 square kilometers) of forest, and killed 57 people.

Mount St. Helens (elevation 8,365 feet / 2,550 meters) and broken stumps on Harry's Ridge—Mount St. Helens National Volcanic Monument, Washington

But the story of Mount St. Helens is not simply one of devastation; it is also one of recovery. Life has slowly returned to the area. Amid broken and toppled trees, squirrels gather seeds, wildflowers bloom, and a new forest spreads across the hills. Even the mountain itself is showing signs of life, with a growing dome at its heart.

Unfortunately we must sometimes face catastrophes, after which there appears to be nothing left and no way to heal. But following the initial shock, we find that while the scars remain, life continues. Like the great mountain, we are forever changed but not forever down.

Earth has no sorrow that earth cannot heal.

—John Muir

Wildflowers surround logs that point to what felled them, Mount St. Helens, with Spirit Lake in between—Mount St. Helens National Volcanic Monument, Washington

Events we deem to be disasters represent mere pages in nature's endless story. Consider the crucial role that wildfires play in the lives of forests, for example. Trees like the lodgepole pine, cypress, and giant sequoia produce cones that can contain hundreds of seeds each. The seeds are held in the cones, which are glued shut by resin. In a forest fire, the resin melts, and the cones open to release their seeds onto a bed of fertile ash, thus allowing the forest to renew itself.

Similarly, while painful events in our lives can be debilitating, they can also trigger renewal. We become stronger when we see loss not only as an end but also as a beginning.

Giant sequoia cone in the Mariposa Grove—Yosemite National Park, California

Nature brims with plants and animals that have adapted to their environment to survive and thrive.

We all face challenges and endure hardship. Our ability to adapt and make the most of our circumstances enables us to succeed.

Bristlecone pine—Mount Evans Recreation Area, Arapaho National Forest, Colorado

Strong winds have caused the tree to have branches on only one side, an effect called *flagging*. The bristlecone pine's adaptability under harsh conditions has allowed it to be among the oldest living things on earth, with some trees having survived thousands of years.

Whether your situation is dire or stable often depends on your point of view. Exploring different vantage points can give you valuable perspective.

Balanced Rock viewed from the north (left) and from the west (right) at sunset—Arches National Park, Utah

Balanced Rock is 128 feet (39 meters) tall, with the balancing rock representing 55 feet (17 meters) of that total.

Perspective includes looking at the big picture. It's easy to become mired in the little problems of daily life. But walking among the giant sequoias of California, some up to three thousand years old, may grant you a different perspective on your comparatively short life and its little problems.

Giant sequoia dwarfs a young pine—Yosemite National Park, California

Giant sequoias, the largest trees in the world by volume, can gain as much as 40 cubic feet (1 cubic meter) of wood per year.

Many plants belonging to the agave and yucca genera spend their lives with an unassuming appearance, their swordlike leaves forming a compact mound. Then, once in the life of one of these plants, it spends all of its stored energy to produce a single, spectacular flower stalk, after which it dies. A well-known example is the century plant (*Agave americana*), which can take twenty to fifty years to produce this single bloom.

You have only one life. Will you go through it quietly, or will you show the world what you can do? Will you waste your energy on trivial matters or put it toward reaching your full potential?

Flowering chaparral yucca on the Big Sur coast—State Route 1, All-American Road, California

The woods can be a dark place, dense with trees whose canopy allows little sunlight to reach the ground. But in early spring, before the deciduous trees have leafed out, the sun illuminates the forest floor, and plants like trillium take advantage of this opportunity to flower.

It often seems that the world is dominated by the big and powerful, but we all have opportunities to blossom.

Trillium—Thompson Wildlife Management Area, Virginia

This area, which is primarily for hunting and fishing, features an exceptionally large stand of trillium that typically flowers in late April and/or early May.

It's easy to take what you have for granted, whether it's health, prosperity, or positive relationships. But making the most of life necessitates seeing the fragility of many of its blessings. When you recognize that something valuable can disappear in an instant, you cherish and enjoy it while you can.

Ephemeral Arch—Valley of Fire State Park, Nevada

This arch lived up to its name. It collapsed in 2010 due to its delicate construction, just a few inches wide on the right side.

Having a plan helps you achieve your goals—but things don't always go according to plan. Rather than stubbornly clinging to it or quitting, you need to have flexibility and the will to find a way.

Life rarely follows a straight line. Success is a process of trying, reacting, and changing.

Determined ponderosa pine—Sunset Crater Volcano National Monument, Arizona

When the main trunk, called a *leader*, was lopped off, perhaps by lightening, a side spur grew to take its place

And as much as we like to be independent, we all need support.

Chapel Rock—Pictured Rocks National Lakeshore, Michigan

The pine atop Chapel Rock is kept alive by the thick roots that anchor it to the land (pictured on the left).

While some cultures celebrate individuality, perhaps the greatest power of an individual lies in the ability to join others to accomplish what only a group can. A single voice cannot make a choir. A single tree cannot make a forest.

Forget-me-nots at the edge of a forest on the Miners Falls Trail—Pictured Rocks National Lakeshore, Michigan

Though many lessons come directly from nature, others come from our interaction with nature, how we explore it, care for it, and appreciate it.

> *Most people who travel look only at what they are directed to look at. Great is the power of the guidebook maker, however ignorant.*
>
> —John Muir

In the photo below, two über photographers stand atop the ridge at the upper right. They have a large format (fancy) camera, use a light meter, and talk in f-stops. Unfortunately they are unaware of this impressive view.

In all endeavors the most important piece of equipment you possess is your head. When you approach the world with curiosity and a willingness to explore, you will see and benefit much more.

Borrego Badlands viewed from near Font's Point at sunrise —Anza–Borrego Desert State Park, California

Many ventures offer no guarantees, and that is frequently true of exploring the outdoors. Will the view be good? Will the waterfall be flowing? Will the wildflowers be blooming? Disappointments can lead to what I call hiker's remorse, where the hiker mutters, "I *knew* I shouldn't have gone on this hike," or, "I could have spent this time on *another* trail." But as often as there are disappointments, there are pleasant surprises, like wildlife sightings. Those fortunate encounters yield special moments that only happen when you take a chance and head out.

Eastern newt (about 2 inches / 5 centimeters long)—Sumter National Forest, South Carolina

Also called the red-spotted newt, the eastern newt has several distinct stages. This salamander is in the eft phase, living on land for up to four years before returning to water as an adult.

And while you're out there, don't forget to see the lighter side of life.

Squirrel on the South Kaibab Trail with O'Neill Butte—Grand Canyon National Park, Arizona

"Uh, excuse me, sir, would you take my picture? The guys back home would never believe I made it here."

Hiking frequently offers a lesson in investing. While some hikes provide interesting scenery from start to finish, many require considerable effort and patience before rewarding the hiker with a vista or landmark. Those who require instant gratification will miss out.

Atlantic coastline—Cutler Coast Public Reserved Land, Maine

A 1.4-mile (2.3-kilometer) trail winds through a forest of spruce and fir trees before reaching the ocean and the rugged shoreline that features bedrock borne of volcanic eruptions 400 million years ago. The trail continues another 3.4 miles (5.5 kilometers) along the rocky coast.

Seasoned hikers (and drivers) know about switchbacks, trails and roads that zigzag gradually up a steep slope to make the ascent easier though longer.

The switchback concept applies to more than just hiking or driving. Whether the goal is career advancement, financial security, or fitness, the surest path is rarely straight to the top. An easy, steady climb generally makes the best approach.

Hiker ascends the switchbacks of the Navajo Loop Trail—Bryce Canyon National Park, Utah

This popular trail takes hikers down from the canyon rim into an area filled with hoodoos named Wall Street.

Which teachers had the greatest impact on you? For many it wasn't the easy ones but the demanding ones because they brought out the best in you. They set the bar high knowing you could reach it, even when *you* weren't sure.

At times nature can be that demanding teacher, directing us to greater heights. When we face the challenge, overcome fear, and push ourselves to achieve, we are rewarded with newfound confidence and an experience to remember.

Left: Angels Landing and the Virgin River; right: Angels Landing viewed from the Angels Landing Trail—Zion National Park, Utah

The last half mile to the summit of Angels Landing follows the narrow "knife-edge" ridge. At some points, chains attached to the rock help hikers hang on. While unsuitable for those with a fear of heights, the intimidating hike looks more difficult than it is. The reward is the view on the next page.

In all excursions, when danger is realized, thought is quick-ened, common care buried, and pictures of wild immortal beauty are pressed into the memory, to dwell forever.

—John Muir

Zion Canyon and the Virgin River (1,390 feet / 424 meters below) viewed from the summit of Angels Landing— Zion National Park, Utah

Although exploring the parks presents many physical challenges, it would be wrong to believe that the benefit of a journey in nature is proportional to its difficulty.

People hike or climb for different reasons, and none could be deemed right or wrong. However, when the trip represents merely a test of skill or endurance, many of the benefits are overlooked because the mind focuses on the task, not the setting.

Parks are not only for those of us who can reach the summits—nature's value is hardly limited to mountaintops. Parks benefit everyone. And those (men) who approach nature with arrogance instead of reverence may fail to reap the rewards available to all who recognize that the greatest journeys are those made with the mind, not the body.

When a mountain is climbed, it is said to be conquered—[may] as well say a man is conquered when a fly [lands] on his head.
—John Muir

Lassen Peak (elevation 13,063 feet / 3,982 meters) and the Painted Dunes—Lassen Volcanic National Park, California

No matter how many parks we visit or peaks we scale, there is always more: more to see, more to feel, and more to learn.

In life, we may strive to reach that one place we believe will deliver ultimate happiness—only to find that once there, we can't stay, that the thrill of living comes not from sitting in a comfortable spot forever but from remaining only long enough to appreciate it and then moving on to pursue the next goal.

Hiker gazes over the Wind River Range from Photographer's Point—Bridger–Teton National Forest, Wyoming

The Wind River Range stretches more than 100 miles (160 kilometers) in western Wyoming and contains 35 named peaks over 13,000 feet (4,000 meters) in elevation.

What do you see pictured below: an elegant great egret, feathers for ladies' hats, or money?

In the late 1800s, feathers from egrets and herons often adorned ladies' hats. Demand for these feathers resulted in the slaughter of thousands of birds.

In 1886 Harriet Hemenway and Minna Hall founded the Audubon Society to halt the trade in feathers and the decimation of the bird population. While the group found some success in outlawing the trade, what ultimately saved the birds was a change in fashion to shorter hairstyles and smaller hats.

As we depend on nature to provide us with the resources we need to live, nature depends on us to act as wise stewards, to protect and preserve it.

Great egret reflects—Everglades National Park, Florida

Many parks seem eternally beautiful. Yet it would be a mistake to take these places for granted since they face many threats, some natural, others manmade. Insects and disease destroy forests. Smog obscures vistas. Climate change melts glaciers. Human development crowds out animal populations. Even heavy park visitation can harm delicate plants and fragile rock formations.

All important relationships, whether with people or nature, require maintenance, with care and understanding.

The Wave of Coyote Buttes North—Vermilion Cliffs National Monument, Arizona

To protect the fragile sandstone formations of this unique area, access is limited to a small number of visitors who must obtain a permit and hike without a trail.

The barbarous notion is almost universally entertained by civilized man, that there is in all the manufactures of Nature something essentially coarse which can and must be eradicated by human culture.

—John Muir

In 1904 Napoleon Bonaparte Broward won Florida's gubernatorial campaign in part by promising to drain the "pestilence-ridden swamp"—the Everglades—to make room for development. Through much of the twentieth century, canals were built to divert the land's water to the ocean. As a result, the Everglades has diminished to less than half its original size, and ninety percent of the wading bird population has vanished.

But the Everglades plays a critical role in flood control and groundwater regulation. The wetlands absorb heavy rain and replenish the underground aquifer, the region's source of drinking water. Efforts to repair the destruction to the ecosystem are now underway.

When we fail to understand the workings and value of nature, we often put ourselves at risk.

Alligator—Everglades National Park, Florida

[A]gain and again, . . . the question comes up: "What are rattlesnakes good for?" As if nothing that does not obviously make for the benefit of man had any right to exist; as if our ways were God's ways. Long ago an Indian to whom a French traveler put this old question replied that their tails were good for toothache, and their heads, for fever. Anyhow, they are all, head and tail, good for themselves, and we need not begrudge them their share of life.

—John Muir

When in the wilderness, we frequently regard native creatures as invaders who threaten us, ones that need to be controlled or killed, when in actuality *they* are threatened by *our* visits to their home.

We share the planet with many roommates, human and animal, and learning about them can turn prejudice and paranoia into understanding and appreciation.

Western fence lizard (about 8 inches / 20 centimeters long)—Joshua Tree National Park, California

Many claim that America's strength lies in its history as a melting pot. But America must take a back seat to the greatest melting pot of all, nature, with its endless variety of flora and fauna all interconnected. To appreciate nature is to celebrate diversity.

When we try to pick out anything by itself, we find it hitched to everything else in the universe.

—John Muir

Great blue heron at Mirror Lake—Blanchard Springs Recreation Area, Ozark National Forest, Arkansas

To enable everyone to fully enjoy nature, we must have respect not only for nature but also for each other.

Linville Falls, one of the most scenic features of North Carolina, attracts tens of thousands of visitors annually. A trail leads to a viewpoint downstream of the thunderous waterfall, from which the photo below was taken.

The view is perfect, provided visitors show restraint by remaining on the trail, unlike the fisherman parked near the base of the waterfall, who fortunately didn't bring a group of buddies, a cooler, and folding chairs.

This particular case is surely no catastrophe; even a fussy photographer could erase the fisherman from a digital photo. But it illustrates the importance of consideration.

The splendor of nature is not a prize to be claimed but a gift to be shared.

Linville Falls (45 feet / 14 meters high)—Blue Ridge Parkway, North Carolina

Having respect for the parks and other visitors goes beyond sharing the view, though.

The canyons of Utah and Arizona, like the one near Devil's Bridge in Sedona, Arizona, can produce impressive echoes. Some people (children and men) like to yell repeatedly (not just once or twice) to hear the echoes, failing to consider that others are there to enjoy nature peacefully.

Acts like yelling (or even talking loudly), littering, taking natural "souvenirs," and carving initials or leaving other graffiti are selfish.

One should take in nature's beauty without taking it away from others.

Devil's Bridge—Coconino National Forest, Arizona

Perhaps nature's greatest lesson is that, just as life can be viewed as a day stone balance, a single day can be seen as a balance of good and bad moments. An encounter with an animal or a golden sunset lasts only a short while, but it reminds us that in the quest for great matter-days and a better life, moments count.

Rocky Mountain bighorn sheep—Mount Evans Recreation Area, Arapaho National Forest, Colorado

Making great matterdays requires the will and patience to find great moments.

I only went out for a walk, and finally concluded to stay out till sundown, for going out, I found, was really going in.
—John Muir

Great egret looks for dinner in the Atlantic Ocean at sunset—Jekyll Island State Park, Georgia

5

Your Experience

Before I started making time in my life to visit America's parks, I was unaware of how magnificent they were. I saw impressive photos and still didn't believe they were *that* good. After all, professional photographers are a tricky bunch. They routinely make moderately attractive celebrities look like flawless supermodels; junk food, like a delicacy. And it seems the grass is always greener—often *much* greener—in postcards. So why shouldn't one expect a certain amount of deception or exaggeration in photos of the parks?

Many scenic photos result from being in the right place at the right time. I would see a park photo and think, "Sure, that's a professional photographer who spent three weeks in the park waiting for the perfect clouds to appear to get this one shot. Or maybe it's some local photographer who went to the park umpteen times before taking this picture."

Lake Alexander just after sunset—Council Grounds State Park, Wisconsin

Let's not forget the equipment. A professional photographer has all manner of lenses and filters—and now computer software—that can distort the perspective and enhance the colors, making everything look better than it actually is. All in the name of artistry, of course.

Fisher Towers (Ancient Art in front of King Fisher) at sunset—Fisher Towers Recreation Site, Utah

Then there are the wildlife pictures, the close-ups of mountain lions and grizzly bears or the shots of exotic and endangered species. "Yeah, right," I would say to myself. "Like I'm gonna see *that*."

In short, I believed those stunning photos didn't represent what *I* would experience during a park visit. I wasn't a photographer on assignment for a magazine; I had a regular job. I didn't have an infinite amount of time to spend in the parks. With a few weeks of vacation each year, I was lucky to spend a couple days in any given park, and I wasn't going to spend my time waiting for the right clouds to appear.

As for any attempt I might make at photography, I was not about to lug around a camera with a lens the size of a bazooka and worth more than my car.

So, although confident that the parks were nice, I doubted that they would appear as fantastic as the photos I had seen would suggest.

Green sea turtle emerges from the ocean—Punalu'u Beach Park, Hawaii County, Hawaii

The endangered green sea turtle, whose name comes from the color of the fat beneath its shell, typically weighs 250 to 450 pounds (113 to 204 kilograms), and its lifespan is estimated to be as long as 80 years.

How wrong I was. The parks really *are* gorgeous in their own right, despite the best efforts of photographers to make me wonder.

The photos in this book were all taken by me. And all but one—the nighttime shot in Joshua Tree National Park—were taken with a compact camera, not a traditional single-lens reflex (SLR) camera.

In most cases, the pictures were taken on the one occasion I was in that spot. Although I did some prior homework to figure out the best times to be in certain places, I didn't spend weeks waiting for the perfect conditions. Unlike a professional photographer on assignment, I couldn't afford to do that. Plus, as a Connecticut resident, I don't have national parks around the corner, such that I could easily make repeated trips.

Palisade Head (rear) and Lake Superior on an early morning in autumn—Tettegouche State Park, Minnesota

Because a photo captures a limited view for a short segment of time, it allows you to focus on a scene in a way that may be difficult with the eyes.

Cascading water of Chittenango Falls—Chittenango Falls State Park, New York

The 167-foot (51-meter) waterfall cascades over roughly 400-million-year-old bedrock.

In so doing, you can find beauty that would otherwise be missed.

Sunshine illuminates the blossoms of a red dogwood—Frelinghuysen Arboretum, Morris County, New Jersey

Photographing something also prompts you to learn about it, further enhancing the memory. After all, you want to know about that plant, animal, or mountain you captured (and that, in turn, captured you).

Swamp lily—Fakahatchee Strand Preserve State Park, Florida

A Florida native, the delicate and fragrant swamp lily grows in wetlands and along streams throughout the state.

OK, so you now know that America's parks offer you spectacular, diverse, and inspiring scenery. But what if you've been to a national park before and didn't have a great matterday?

Maybe you went to the Grand Canyon, like so many have. You stopped at a viewpoint and said, "Wow." You had your picture taken, as if you had just met a celebrity, cozying up to imply some level of familiarity that doesn't exist. You went to the gift shop and bought a T-shirt.

Grand Canyon viewed from the South Rim at sunset—Grand Canyon National Park, Arizona

The park receives over four million recreational visits per year.

Now, there's no need to get defensive; neither you nor your loved ones are being indicted for incorrect park behavior. You needn't feel guilty about stopping for a quick snapshot at a viewpoint and driving away, or lingering in a park gift shop, which almost all visitors do.

The intent here is not to establish right and wrong ways to enjoy nature but rather to show that there are *different* ways, and what you do can have a dramatic impact on your experience. And that experience can, in turn, have a dramatic impact on you.

Vernal Fall (317 feet / 97 meters high) and hikers on the Mist Trail—Yosemite National Park, California

Many people subscribe to the popular notion that the best parks belong on a list of places to see before they die, equating these parks with famous tourist destinations like the Eiffel Tower. By that thinking, a single visit at any point in one's life suffices.

However, the day stone balance tells a different story. Great matter-days remain on the day stone balance, affecting your life on the day they occur and every day thereafter. So the earlier they happen, the better; waiting means potentially sacrificing years or even decades of benefit. Plus, the quality of your experience may suffer if you become physically less capable of exploring. Obviously responsibilities may prevent you from visiting parks whenever you wish, but what's important to know is that timing matters.

Also, a single visit to a park may satisfy those who view the parks like must-see classic movies to be crossed off their to-do lists. But when you see the parks as friends, you recognize that every visit is unique, that you can have different experiences depending on what you choose to do together and what occurs during the visits.

Point Imperial (left) and Mount Hayden (right)—Grand Canyon National Park, Arizona

Ninety percent of visits to Grand Canyon National Park are to the South Rim, but the North Rim offers plenty of scenic treasures, including this view.

Still, even with all the incentives, you may have perfectly valid reasons for not going outside at all.

It's too hot.

Lighthouse formation (75 feet / 23 meters tall)—Palo Duro Canyon State Park, Texas

It's too cold.

Frozen Kaaterskill Falls (260 feet / 79 meters high)—Kaaterskill Wi d Forest, Catskill Park, New York

It's too early.

Sun rises over bald cypresses in Bluff Lake—Noxubee National Wildlife Refuge, Mississippi

It's getting late.

Lake Champlain and New York's Adirondack Mountains at dusk—Mount Philo State Park, Vermont

There are wild animals out there.

Sika deer (Asian elk)—Assateague Island National Seashore, Maryland

Sika deer were introduced to Assateague Island in the 1920s, imported from their native Japan.

There are scary places.

Manly Beacon (right) viewed from Zabriskie Point—Death Valley National Park, California

While daunting as the continent's hottest and driest place, Death Valley offers colorful badlands, sand dunes, mesmerizing salt flats, snowy mountain peaks, and occasional explosions of wildflowers.

You could get lost.

Endless dunes—White Sands National Monument, New Mexico

This park's gypsum dunes cover 275 square miles (712 square kilometers). As the water from an ephemeral lake evaporates, gypsum deposits are left behind to be carried away by the wind, eventually forming dunes.

Or maybe you'd rather just stay in.

Black-tailed prairie dogs—Theodore Roosevelt National Park, North Dakota

These highly social animals live in colonies known as prairie dog "towns" that can be as large as hundreds of acres (hectares) and contain thousands of individuals.

Perhaps you think the parks are too far away. The photos in this book include all fifty states to show that you don't have to travel to exotic places halfway around the globe to experience nature at its finest, and reap the rewards of doing so. The scenery doesn't necessarily improve in proportion to how far you travel or how much you spend.

To the sane and free, it will hardly seem necessary to cross the continent in search of wild beauty, however easy the way, for they find it in abundance wherever they chance to be.

—John Muir

Travertine Creek—Chickasaw National Recreation Area, Oklahoma

Even if the best parks are out of reach (geographically or finan-cially), nature still delivers many of its wonders to you daily, in the form of the sun, the moon, the clouds, and—depending on your location and the season—flowers, trees, bodies of water, and even snow. You have only to look.

Tallgrass prairie—Konza Prairie Preserve, Kansas

This preserve, which is open to the public, is owned and maintainec by The Nature Conservancy and Kansas State University.

The East is blessed with good winters and blossoming clouds that shed white flowers over all the land, covering every scar and making the saddest landscape divine at least once a year.
—John Muir

Kettletown Brook after a snowstorm—Kettletown State Park, Connecticut

Consider how lucky you are to live in this time. You can research a park on the Internet, fly to the nearest city, drive a rental car to the park, watch an introductory video in the visitor center, and then experience the park firsthand on maintained trails with interpretive signs. John Muir didn't have those benefits. While he certainly saw some parks in a more natural state, he could never visit all the places available to you.

Moss-draped maples of the Hoh Rain Forest—Olympic National Park, Washington

The Hoh Rain Forest receives 140 to 170 inches (356 to 432 centimeters) of precipitation each year.

Plus, the accessibility of today's parks means that great matterdays in nature are hardly limited to the young and energetic. Even those with limited mobility can enjoy spectacular scenery.

As age comes on, one source of enjoyment after another is closed, but Nature's sources never fail. Like a generous host, she offers her brimming cups in endless variety, served in a grand hall, the sky its ceiling, the mountains its walls, decorated with glorious paintings and enlivened with bands of music ever playing.

—John Muir

The Alaskan taiga displays fall color from shrub birch and willow, as seen from the park road—Denali National Park & Preserve, Alaska

Denali is 6,000,000 acres (242,811 hectares) of wilderness bisected by one road, most of which is accessible by shuttle or tour bus only.

Still, the greatest rewards come to those who can explore the parks on foot.

While many people seek motivation to exercise or lose weight, the parks provide a straightforward incentive: when you're able to hike, you can see more and experience nature without the distraction of crowds.

Ganoga Falls (94 feet / 29 meters high)—Ricketts Glen State Park, Pennsylvania

Ricketts Glen features 22 named waterfalls, 21 of which can be seen on the 7.2-mile (11.6-kilometer) Falls Trail. The park was slated to become a national park, but the onset of World War II ended that development plan.

If you feel that you don't have time to spend in parks like these, consider the time as being not merely spent but invested.

The time will not be taken from the sum of your life. Instead of shortening, it will indefinitely lengthen it and make you truly immortal. Nevermore will time seem short or long, and cares will never again fall heavily on you, but gently and kindly as gifts from heaven.

—John Muir

Canyon of the Blackwater River in early autumn, viewed from Lindy Point—Blackwater Falls State Park, West Virginia

That investment of time yields more than just the great matterdays spent in nature. The effects of these great matterdays radiate to the days of excited planning and eager anticipation beforehand and to the days of looking at photos and recounting experiences afterward. One visit to a park can result in many stones on the positive side of the day stone balance.

Devils Tower (867 feet / 264 meters tall) takes on a golden hue at sunset—Devils Tower National Monument, Wyoming

Devils Tower was formed from molten magma forced upward into sedimentary rocks followed by the gradual erosion of the surrounding rocks.

Of course, free time is not always completely free. For example, the responsibilities that come with having a family can present challenges to those wanting to explore nature. At the same time, though, nature provides opportunities for parents to share experiences, teach lessons, and see the world through youthful eyes.

Mother and son share a morning near the Otter Cliffs—Acadia National Park, Maine

Acadia, with its unique landscape sculpted by glaciers, became the first national park east of the Mississippi River in 1919.

Naturally how you spend your time is a personal decision affected by taste and practical constraints, but that decision should be an informed one. Unfortunately, the benefits of nature are not taught in school. And, as I noted earlier, nature doesn't advertise. Sometimes the appreciation of nature is passed from previous generations, but too often it isn't. So this book's goal is to act as nature's brochure and help you to see the potential rewards of spending time in nature.

The Cascades (66 feet / 20 meters high) and Little Stony Creek—Jefferson National Forest, Virginia

Even if you have some free time to invest, you could rightly claim that touring all these places is neither a small nor an inexpensive venture. But the idea is not for you to visit every park in this book, see the same things, and make the same observations. The experience must be your own. You would undoubtedly find your own special places and moments and messages.

My hope is that you experience the same positive effect on your life that John Muir and I have enjoyed. It's impossible to guarantee that outcome, of course, but you should at least be aware of that potential. If you can pile up some stones on the right end of your day stone balance, you may find that the quality of your life has improved.

Hiker views Corona Arch (opening 105 feet / 32 meters high)—Corona Arch Trail, Utah

While hundreds of thousands of visitors flock to Arches National Park annually, plenty of spectacular arches may be seen elsewhere in Utah and nearby Colorado. This arch lies just a few miles outside the national park, near the city of Moab, Utah.

6

Will You?

We've all heard this expression, or some variation, numerous times: "Sh-t happens."

I understand the sentiment—we all do. There's no denying that things can and do go wrong. But I'd like to offer you a more positive view that deserves equal time: beauty happens.

When your path through life has you bouncing between the same familiar places, experiences, and emotions, it's easy to overlook the gifts of nature. But they should not be missed. If you go outside, you may come to agree.

Yes, indeed, beauty happens.

It happens day . . .

Sunlight illuminates a red maple displaying peak autumn color—Sleep ng Giant State Park, Connecticut

... and night.

Aurora borealis (the northern lights)—Chena Lake Recreation Area, Fairbanks North Star Borough, Alaska

The aurora occurs when solar wind particles, traveling along the earth's magnetic field lines, collide with atoms in the earth's atmosphere.

It's happening right now.

Rock House—Hocking Hills State Park, Ohio

This sandstone cave is 200 feet (61 meters) long and has a ceiling 25 feet (8 meters) high. Iron compounds add color to the rock walls.

It happens from coast . . .

Face Rock (upper left) and sea stacks at sunset—Face Rock State Scenic Viewpoint, Oregon

. . . to coast . . .

Sunset over the mouth of Narragansett Bay—Brenton Point State Park, Rhode Island

. . . and in countless places in between.

Sandstone formations on the shores of Wilson Lake—Rocktown Natural Area, Wilson Lake, Kansas

It happens in big cities . . .

Flowering dogwood—U.S. National Arboretum, Washington, D.C.

. . . and remote places.

Zebra Slot Canyon—Grand Staircase–Escalante National Monument, Utah

It happens in famous parks . . .

American Falls (188 feet / 57 meters high)—Niagara Falls State Park, New York

Between American Falls and neighboring Bridal Veil Falls and Horseshoe Falls, over 3,160 tons (2,867 tonnes) of water flow over the falls every second.

. . . and ones little known.

Anderson Falls (12 feet / 4 meters high)—Anderson Falls Park, Bartholomew County, Indiana

It happens in grand places . . .

Grand Canyon of the Yellowstone and Lower Yellowstone Falls (308 feet / 94 meters high) viewed from Artist Point—Yellowstone National Park, Wyoming

. . . and small.

Ladybug on a daffodil—Hubbard Park, Meriden, Connecticut

It happens near you.

Glory Hole (31-foot / 9-meter waterfall through a hole into a grotto)—Ozark National Forest, Arkansas

Will you be there?

Hiker enjoys the view—Garden of the Gods Recreation Area, Shawnee National Forest, Illinois

Will you take the time to appreciate your world . . .

Photographer awaits sunrise—Bryce Canyon National Park, Utah

. . . and all of its inhabitants?

White ibises walk the beach—Bowman's Beach, Sanibel, Lee County, Florida

The ibis uses its long, curved bill to probe for food in water or loose soil.

Will you feel the *awezure*?

Couple views the badlands at the White River Valley Overlook—Badlands National Park, South Dakota

Will you hear nature's inspirational messages?

Hiker admires the President, a 3,200-year-old giant sequoia—Sequoia National Park, California

The President, named for President Warren G. Harding in 1923, is 247 feet (75 meters) tall and 27 feet (8 meters) in diameter, and it possesses nearly two billion leaves.

Will you come to see that the quality of your life is determined by the choices you make, that you have the power to decide where your day stones end up?

Red granite boulders dwarf a visitor—Elephant Rocks State Park, Missouri

Will you occasionally escape the rut of everyday life to pursue great matterdays, ones whose impact will remain with you and make a positive difference in your life?

Hiker looks over the Black Hills from atop Little Devils Tower—Custer State Park, South Dakota

Go outside.

Couple hikes the Taggart Lake Trail beneath Grand Teton (elevation 13,770 feet / 4,197 meters) and Mount Owen (elevation 12,928 feet / 3,940 meters)—Grand Teton National Park, Wyoming

For more photos and park information
plus travel and photography resources,
visit the companion website for this book:
GoOutsideBook.com

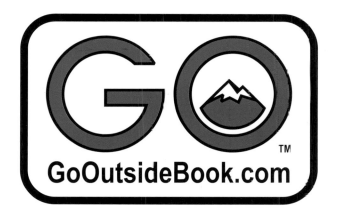

Index